HOW TO READ FASTER

DOUBLE YOUR READING SPEED, IMPROVE COMPREHENSION AND RETAIN MORE OF EVERYTHING YOU READ

STEVEN HOPKINS

CONTENTS

INTRODUCTION

If you're reading this book, you are clearly someone who is interested in learning to read faster. Of course, you have your own reasons. It could be that you want to study faster and smarter for school, or a course at work. It could be that you are keen to do a better job in your day to day activities that involve taking in a large amount of information. It could be as simple as joining a book club and needing to read a new book every week in order to talk about it with authority. Whatever your reasons, it is important to know that if you are committed to learning to read faster, I can help you to do just that.

What gives me the ability to tutor you on reading faster? Well, I myself have had to go through the process of learning to read faster. It's not that I was a particularly slow reader, but we all go through changes in life and I found myself needing to push myself to learn faster in order to keep up with my evolving situation at work and at home. I'm sure the same is true of you. Just because you are reading this book, it doesn't mean that you are particularly slow at reading, or slow at anything. Remember that there is nothing to be ashamed about in reading a book like this. Like I said before, you have your own reasons for wanting to read faster, and I respect those reasons.

Your desire to read faster doesn't necessarily need to mean that you are slow in any way, shape or form. To me it just means that you want to get better at something, and in this case that something is reading. That's right, this book will not only help you to read faster, but it will also teach you to be an all around better reader. At this stage you may be wondering how someone can be a better reader. "Surely, you either understand the words you're reading or you don't, how can you be a better reader?" Well, learning to read more quickly is only part of what you really want. You may say that you want to learn to read faster, but what you also need to do is to learn to take in that information that you are reading, understand it and retain it. After all, what's the use of reading really quickly if you're not going to understand what you've been reading and not going to remember it?

Again, there is nothing to be ashamed about in looking for some help to improve your reading speed and skills. On the contrary, you should be commended for actively trying to improve yourself. As humans it is in our nature to continue learning and broadening our horizons. The fact that you are reading this book and pushing yourself to be a better person is a testament to that most human of characteristics.

I respect your desire to be a better reader and refine your skills. Perhaps I find it easier to respect your determination because I have gone through the same thing. Like I said before, I have never been a particularly slow reader, or a particularly fast reader either. Since my earliest days at school, I have just been an average person reading at an average speed. Maybe that's why I love sharing my experiences so much. I am an average guy who has had gone through a lot of disappointments, but I have also used the knowledge gathered from those failures to fuel some significant successes that have set me and my family up for life. Now I want you to use my experiences and knowledge to benefit your endeavours in life. This is why I write these books, it's a joy seeing you take my knowledge and create your own successes from it.

My need to read faster came from my need to learn more and advance my career. I had been working a dead end job when a chance encounter with Linda Vale, the woman who would become my mentor and life coach. We got to chatting on the train and she opened my eyes to how complacent I had become working my desk job. I had put on weight and had nothing to look forward to at the end of each day, except for a frozen microwave meal and playing video games. Linda helped me to see that I needed more in my life. I actually believe that I already knew it when I met Linda, but she was the catalyst I needed to make some changes.

Thanks to Linda I started getting into shape. I went to the gym and began working out. Before long I was a gym bunny, something I had never thought I would ever be. This is what led to me seriously considering switching to being a full time personal trainer. It took a while, in fact it took more than a while. It took dedication and commitment to my goals. Being a personal fitness trainer is more than just looking the part. I had to learn a lot about nutrition, the human body, and common ailments. That took a lot of reading on my part and that is where I first began to realize that I wanted to read faster. It was not only important that I read faster, but I had to truly absorb the information I was reading and be able to demonstrate my understanding of it if I was to gain my certificates as a qualified personal fitness trainer.

Some time later and I had my certificates in hand. My journey to learning to read faster didn't end there. This is because it is true that we never really stop learning, but I certainly didn't stop my personal development by becoming a fitness instructor. Before long I had a small family to take care of and I desperately wanted to boost my income in order to provide what they needed and give them a good quality of life. This meant a lot more reading and a whole bunch of adventures along the way!

What is really fascinating to me, and I hope it will be for you, is how engrossing yourself in learning one particular skill always spreads to enhance other areas of your life. Some of my skills as a personal trainer have become central to the way I live my life. For example, that never give up attitude that I developed as a trainer became vital when I was pitching different ideas for products and businesses to investors. So it is with learning to read faster.

I have found that the skills developed in reading

faster have not only allowed me to save time and get more done, but they have improved my concentration and focus so I can really read with greater depth. Along with better reading skills comes greater levels of creativity and problem solving skills. You may have picked up this book to help with academic study, but you will find that the skills this book encourages you to develop will be with you for the rest of your life, helping you to secure the promotions you deserve and live the life that you want for yourself, and your family. I know that with commitment to the lessons we go through here, you are going to achieve great things. Stick with me and you'll soon discover that you will learn and achieve far more than you had bargained for. Your journey is just starting, let's take it together!

Chapter 1

GETTING STARTED

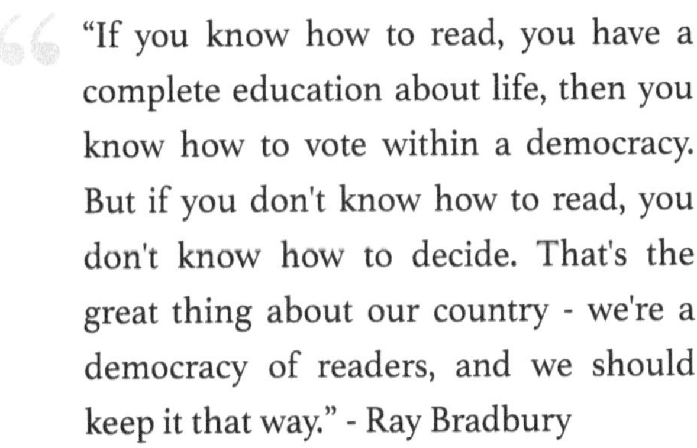

> "If you know how to read, you have a complete education about life, then you know how to vote within a democracy. But if you don't know how to read, you don't know how to decide. That's the great thing about our country - we're a democracy of readers, and we should keep it that way." - Ray Bradbury

I f you're going to learn how to read quicker, you first need to understand why some of us read slowly. There are many reasons that explain why we do this and this chapter is all about getting you in the right headspace before you begin your journey to becoming a faster and more effective reader. Before we start jumping into the nitty gritty we need to begin by getting you prepared so you are in the best possible place to absorb the knowledge that the forthcoming chapters will bring you.

It is always best to read the instructions before putting up some flat pack furniture, and this is no different. Like assembling flat pack furniture, you need to have all the necessary tools at hand before you start. I know that you are eager to begin digging into the good stuff, but stick with me through this chapter and we'll soon get to the essential exercises that will have you reading quicker in no time.

Understanding why we read slowly

It is important that we understand the reasons why some of us tend to read slower than others. As mentioned before, there are lots of reasons why this may be the case, and this chapter will take us through the different things that stop us from reading as quickly as we can. As I said in the intro-duction, it is not necessarily that we are particularly slow at reading. Often there are things that get in the way of us reading at the speed we are able to. So let's go through these things so we can begin to identify them in our behaviour and hopefully avoid them in the future. As well as learning excellent new techniques for quicker reading, it is very important that we identify bad habits that get in our way, so we can discard these old habits.

Vocalizing

Vocalizing whilst reading is simply when you read the words out loud, instead of reading silently, in your head. If you're someone who does this, it is nothing to be ashamed of, it is just one of those bad habits that you picked up, probably whilst still at school when you were learning to read, and never let go of it. When we're small we all learn to read by reading out loud, but it is a crutch that most of us let go. Some of us don't let go of this crutch, even though we are very capable readers and no longer have any use for vocalizing.

Vocalizing may hinder your ability to read with speed by requiring you to read every single word out loud. This has an impact on the speed with which you can read. If you want to become a speed reader this is a habit that you need to break. Don't get me wrong, everybody vocalizes a little, but the less you vocalize, the better. Additionally, it has been claimed by some that vocalizing can hinder our ability to understand what we are reading. How is this possible? Because by concentrating on moving our lips, we're engaging part of our minds that should be concentrating on understanding the text that we are reading.

Ditching vocalisation means that you can understand entire sentences with one or two glances rather than focusing on each word as it comes. Ironically, we understand more when we read faster. One could be forgiven for believing the opposite to be true, but that's just how it goes.

Negative mind-wandering

Our minds wander during all sorts of tasks, not only when we are reading. But why does that happen and what is occurring within our minds when it does happen? Well, as far as what is happening in our brains is concerned, neurons begin to run out of fuel after only 12 seconds of serious effort when we're performing a task. When this happens they look for lactate, a sugar. If lactate is not found, they look for glycogen. If that can't be found either, they become tired and allow other parts of our brain to get our attention, and this is when our minds wander.

Researchers have found that our minds wander less when we are doing something that we are good at, and more when it is something that requires more effort. If our minds wander it is usually at the expense of our performance at the task we are engaged in. Reading is one of the biggest tasks that can be impacted by our inability to concentrate. Specifically it is impacted by our lack of reading comprehension. The same issues arise for attention span and problem-solving tasks. Children who allow their minds to wander tend to perform more poorly and may end up diagnosed with an attention deficit.

Positive mind-wandering

A wandering mind does not need to be all bad, however. If you're one of those people whose mind does tend to wander on tasks, then you will be glad to know that a wandering mind can actually be a good thing. Research has shown that a wandering mind can be a sign that you are able to think about several things at once - *high capacity working memory.*

This means that your brain naturally makes resources available for the most pressing tasks or problems it needs to solve, an excellent thing when it comes to planning, but still quite destructive when it comes to concentrating on what you're reading.

Jumping Back

This phenomenon goes by several different terms, *jumping back* being just one of them. It also goes by:

- Back-skipping
- Re-reading
- Regression
- and others...

Ok, so we know some of the different terms for it, but what does it actually mean? As you may have already guessed, jumping back refers to the habit of going back over text that you have already read. It is estimated that people who do *jump back* waste about a third of all the time they spend reading in this way. Not only that but it is a huge knock to your concentration because those who regress are interrupting the natural flow of information. Some of us re-read just a few lines, or a paragraph, if it's a passage in a novel or an article that we really enjoyed. However, some people re-read entire pages, or even chapters when they really don't need to.

Why do people *jump back*? They don't trust their ability to comprehend what they are reading, so they tend to re-read things to make sure that they have understood. But why do they feel this way? Well, because they really haven't understood everything to their satisfaction. Why not? Because they keep interrupting the flow of their reading to re-read things they have already read. Their belief that they need to re-read things leads to them not comprehending what they read.

Methods to improve your reading speed

Of course, there are lots of methods you can use and techniques you can develop to speed up your reading, many of which we are going to be explored in some detail in the forthcoming chapters. But here are a few to get you started because I know that you are eager to feel like you are achieving something.

Initial Speed Reading

First, before you begin anything you need to have an accurate understanding of how quickly, or slowly, you read. Find yourself a stopwatch, perhaps use the timer app on your smartphone, and get it ready to count down from sixty seconds. Also, get a page ready from a book. Get the timer counting down and start reading the page. When the timer sounds the alarm for sixty seconds stop reading and make a note of the exact word you reached on the page. Now, begin counting the words you have read. When you have that figure you will have your words per minute read speed.

Alternatively you can perform an online search for read speeds. You will find many online resources for reading tests with apps on web pages that can time your reading for you, and give you your words per minute at the end of the test.

Trackers and Pacers

You may have heard of the Pointer method, or even if you don't know that it is called the Pointer method, you will surely know the method itself. The Pointer method is simply running the tip of your finger beneath the line you are reading. Using trackers and pacers is similar to the Pointer method. However, the key difference with trackers and pacers is that it is a big help in avoiding regression. Instead of using your finger tip, as you would with the Pointer method, you use a pen, or a pencil, to underline the line you are reading as you go along. This will not only help to focus your concentration, but it will also remind you of the lines that you have already read.

Expand Peripheral Vision

Expand your peripheral vision to allow yourself to take in more visual information. This is particularly useful when you are reading to take in information, not just reading for pleasure. This method, usually by scanning down the center of a page, will allow you to read most of the words so you get the gist of what you are reading. Your brain will pick up on particular words, key phrases and entire sentences, usually at the beginning and ending of paragraphs to give you the essential information without getting bogged down with superfluous words. Using this method you will process more at a time.

What We've Learned

- Vocalizing is the habit of voicing the words you're reading.
- Your mind wanders when you're working on something that demands extra effort.
- Having a wandering mind isn't necessarily a bad thing, but it does mean that you're not concentrating on reading.
- Jumping back, or regression, is another habit that can slow you down when you're reading.
- Perform a simple test to determine your words per minute speed.
- Use the tracker and pacer method of underlining lines you have read to prevent regression.
- Expand your peripheral vision and scan the page to take in more essential information at once.

Chapter 2

WHAT IS SPEED READING?

"I do think digital media encourages speed-reading, which can be fine if one is simply seeking information. But a serious novel or work of history or volume of poetry is an experience one should savor, take time over." - Michael Dirda

Ok, so we have already gone over some basic techniques that you can work into your reading routine to make yourself a quicker reader, but before we dive any further into the world of speed reading, just what is speed reading anyway? Yes, the clue may be in the term and it is easy to surmise that it is to do with reading with speed. But what exactly is meant by that, how did it originate, when was it devised, what were the theories that underpinned this idea and how have they evolved over time?

Don't worry, we're not going to go into too much detail, but it is always good to know the origins of particular theories. In learning more about theories that can help our lives we can understand more about them and picture how we can incorporate them into our lives. By learning more about speed reading we can figure out how best to adopt the various techniques that we will be discussing. In learning about the origins of speed reading you can select the techniques that will be the best fit for your lifestyle, learner type, and what you really want to achieve from speed reading.

Brief history of speed reading

Evelyn Wood, who died in 1995, is generally known as being the one who came up with the term *speed reading*. But she didn't only come up with the term, she promoted the idea that reading is a skill that could be improved, not just a question of being able to read, or not.

She became interested in the 1940s as a teacher at a high school in Salt Lake City, Utah, in the US. Evelyn observed how underachieving students struggled with even the simplest tasks and became convinced that their poor reading skills were the cause of all their issues.

She started a remedial program from her school and proved her hypothesis correct. Once they began improving their reading skills, they improved in other areas of their academic studies. Once they became suitably proficient in reading, Ms. Wood encouraged the students to read faster, discovering that faster reading led to better understanding of what they were reading. This is the discovery that led her to work on speed reading.

It was some years later that Ms. Wood, studying for a master's degree at university, discovered that one of her professors, Dr. Lees, could read at a rate of 2,500 words per minute. She discovered this when he read her entire 80-page term paper, marked it and returned it to her within a few minutes while she watched, stunned.

Ms. Wood went on to study other fast readers in order to identify their traits, eventually talking to 53 superfast readers and leading to her own reading skills business with 150 bases. In 1959 Evelyn started Evelyn Wood Reading Dynamics and US presidents Kennedy, Nixon and Carter ended up sending members of their administrations to learn from her.

How speed reading has progressed

We already discussed Evelyn Wood who had the first serious impact on bringing speed reading to a significant audience and made the theory known in households around the world. How about some of the other important people?

Emil Javel conducted the first scientific analysis around 1878 into how the eyes are capable of seeing, reading and processing not just a single word at a time, but groups of words.

. . .

In 1894 The Education Review began its investigation into how effective it would be to teach people to read groups of words without vocalizing.

John O'Brian in 1921 developed the first theory on silent reading skills. His idea was to use eye fixation without vocalizing to encourage our brains to see, read and process groups of words at a time.

1980 saw Jan Davidson develop the first example of an interactive software program to teach speed reading. The program was called the Ultimate Speed Reader.

Foundations of Speed Reading

Now let's go over some of the things that form the basis of speed reading, the basics that are part and parcel of any speed reading course. The next few items in this section are the building blocks that have formed part of the theory of speed reading for as long as it has existed. Reading multiple words, subvocalization, and skipping words are techniques that most speed readers develop for themselves and continue to improve over time. If you want to be a speed reader with the best of them, then these are some techniques that you have to get to know, and habits that you need to try to adopt.

Reading multiple words at a time

This is a big deal in speed reading and there are many people out there who either read like this, or claim they can read like this. There is even a theory that people can read several lines at a time within the sweep of their vision as they cast their eyes from left to right. Probably the most extreme example of this is the late Kim Peek, the man who served as inspiration for the character Rain Man, or Raymond, played by Dustin Hoffman in the movie Rain Man. Peek was born without a connection between the two hemispheres of his brain, so it is possible that they worked independently, to an extent. This means that he could read two pages at a time and each hemisphere processed the information simultaneously.

Removing subvocalization

Vocalization is when we say out loud each word we are reading. Subvocalization is how we silently pronounce the word that we are reading. Yes, even if we are silently pronouncing the word it does slow us down, as mentioned before. This is because we are not only taking the time to pronounce the word, but we are also allocating vital resources to the pronunciation of these words, instead of distributing them where they are needed most, in the reading of the words.

Most speed reading courses will say that eliminating subvocalization from your reading habit is necessary if you are going to become a speed reader. In fact it is one of the most basic things that you can instantly try to do, however it will not be easy. Studies have shown that even the fastest speed readers continue to subvocalize and it is, to an extent, necessary.

Learning to skip words

Again, I mentioned this earlier, but it is worth mentioning again because it is so fundamental to your campaign and efforts to become a faster reader. Skipping words does not sound like a good thing to do, especially if you are studying something that very much depends on knowing your facts and getting things right. However, in any text there will be words that may be considered surplus to your requirements.

. . .

It's not that these words do not have meaning or don't hold the ability to change the meaning of a sentence. It is just that, as far as your visual field is concerned, you only need the key words and key phrases in order to make sense of what you are reading, the rest of it is simply unnecessary in this context. You can learn to train your brain to pick out the essential information from each piece of text that you read.

Difference between speed reading and normal reading

Efficient readers VS inefficient readers

Efficient readers are those who read a passage a single time and don't regress to read it again needlessly. Inefficient readers are those who need to jump back every so often, but they are also those who lack the necessary concentration to continue with their reading without giving in to distractions. Also efficient readers are those who are able to absorb the information from what they are reading and retain it.

Why do some people read faster and others very slow?

The differences between fast readers and slow readers vary, but generally it comes down to how we learned to read as children. As children, we all picked up bad habits here and there. Some of us carry those bad habits into our adult years, such as vocalisation. For others it is the lack of concentration that hampers our ability to read as quickly as we can. For many people a negative attitude towards reading, that they developed as children, has contributed to how they view reading as adults, so they try to do it as little as possible. This in turn means that they read more slowly because they don't recognize the words as quickly. Quickly recognizing words means that we can skip them without really reading them.

What We've Learned

- Evelyn Wood coined the term speed reading.
- She discovered the link between poor reading skills amongst students and an overall improvement in their grades in all

subjects when they improved those reading skills.

- It is possible to read multiple words at a time to speed up your reading.
- Eliminating subvocalization is not entirely possible but you can reduce it.
- Skipping unnecessary words can help you to read faster.
- Efficient readers read a passage once and have better concentration levels.
- Negative childhood habits and attitudes can influence how we view reading as adults.

Chapter 3

MINDSET & PREPARATION

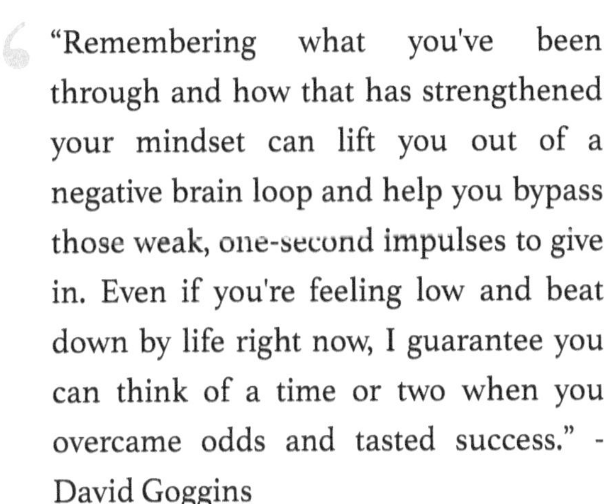

"Remembering what you've been through and how that has strengthened your mindset can lift you out of a negative brain loop and help you bypass those weak, one-second impulses to give in. Even if you're feeling low and beat down by life right now, I guarantee you can think of a time or two when you overcame odds and tasted success." - David Goggins

If you are going to embark upon a journey towards becoming a better and faster reader, you need to make sure that you are ready for the challenge. This means being prepared so you stand as good a chance as possible of making it to your goals. If you are serious about achieving all that you want, it is vital that you prepare. The best and most accomplished explorers didn't set out on their adventures without doing their research, gathering their maps and plotting a route. You are no different.

This is an exciting adventure that you are embarking upon, and you need to have the correct outlook. This means planning and preparing, taking on the right mindset that will ensure your success, and this is what we are discussing this chapter.

The importance of speed comprehension

We usually understand one hundred percent of everything that we read when we read at our normal speed of around 200 to 400 words per minute. It has been argued that speed reading leads our comprehension to take a nosedive. To an extent, this can be true, but with practice comes an enhanced ability to understand whilst speed reading.

As mentioned before, there is no point in being able to read super fast if you're not going to understand what you are actually reading. If you're taking the time to read something, then it must be worth understanding. So don't neglect to actually absorb the information you are reading. When you're reading more complex material it may be more difficult to fully grasp what is being explained in the text, while other, simpler texts will be more easily understood.

It is vital that you understand what you are reading. A good tip is to practice your speed reading early in the morning. As part of your practice, try to create a mental image of the information from the text. The brain is better at sorting visual information, so it will work better with a picture of the text, than it does with the text itself. Of course, the most important thing is that you continue to practice because that is the only way that you will get better at understanding what you are speed reading.

Learn to read ideas, instead of just the words

This might sound like the kind of advice Yoda would give to young Luke, but it is not that difficult to understand. Yes, the ideas contained within a text are made up of the words, because that is how text works. You can't absorb the information being communicated via the text without the words, but I'm not asking you to abandon the words.

Keep reading the words, at least for now, but begin training yourself to also consider the idea that the words are trying to communicate. Don't wait until you get to the end of the sentence, or the paragraph, before you begin assimilating all the details. If you begin to consider the idea whilst you are actually reading you will find that it makes more sense. As it makes more sense, you will find that you are reading more quickly.

A way to do this is to skim read to pick up the key words and phrases. This way you will be starting to skip the unnecessary words, as discussed earlier, focusing your energies on only the words that really matter.

Develop visual and conceptual thinking skills

As mentioned above, the brain is better able to process images than it does words, so thinking in terms of images and concepts is a way of taking short cuts around the words on the page. What does this mean? Well, this means either thinking with pictures in combination with words, or thinking exclusively in pictures or visual tools, such as charts and flowcharts. Organizing information in this way means that you spend less energy visualizing words and more on creating more easily understood images.

Believe you can read faster

Before you do anything else you need to be able to see yourself speed reading. Yes, you need to win the psychological battle and believe that you can be *one of those people* who can speed read. There is no reason why you can't and I believe that you can do anything as long as you have the right attitude and commit to practicing as much as you can. As with any skill, you will only get better at speed reading if you practice.

What you need to practice speed reading

The first thing you need is time and a quiet place to practice. Ideally a place with as few distractions as possible. If this is impossible at home, try booking a private reading room at your local library. There usually isn't a fee for this and it means that you will have your own stall free from the distractions of any TV sets. Also, switch off your smartphone so you don't have any notifications to distract you. Start with a simple text that you can practice with, something that isn't loaded with complex ideas. Maybe something corny from the romance section of the library. As you get better you can progress to something more complex. To begin with the most important things you need are time, solitude, a place free of distractions, and something simple to practice with.

What We've Learned

- Try to create a mental image of what you are reading as the brain works better with images than words.
- Think about what you're reading as you're reading it.

- Try to learn to think in images as this cuts down the time spent on words.
- Win the mental battle and believe that you can read faster.
- Find time, solitude, a place without distractions, and a simple text to start practicing.

Chapter 4

LIGHTENING SPEED-READING TECHNIQUES

"Reading and writing, like everything else, improve with practice. And, of course, if there are no young readers and writers, there will shortly be no older ones. Literacy will be dead, and democracy - which many believe goes hand in hand with it - will be dead as well." - Margaret Atwood

If you're keen on becoming a top notch speed reader, you will have to familiarize yourself with the techniques that will eventually, with effort and dedication, become skills. Right now it might seem like an unattainable dream, something far off and difficult to imagine for yourself. But the whole reason that you are reading this book is that you are not someone who gives up easily. No, instead you're the sort of person who dares to dream of bigger and better things for yourself and that is why you are committing yourself to putting in the effort and time to make yourself a more accomplished person.

You should be proud of yourself, even when you think that this is all going to be too much for you and you feel like giving up. We all get like that from time to time and it is only natural when you're trying to do something that will be worth your time and effort, that you feel a little overwhelmed. Anything that is worth doing will be difficult, and anything that is difficult will be occasionally overwhelming.

The most important thing is that you don't give in, you don't listen to those negative voices. Negativity can bring you down, not just from those around you who may be secretly jealous that you are trying to better yourself, but also from within you. That negative voice inside your head is one that you need to ignore if you are going to achieve your goals.

. . .

Read on and let's take a closer look at the techniques that will support you as you take on speed reading, and win!

How to improve focus and concentration

Multitasking is an inevitable consequence of modern living. With all of our tablets, laptops, work phones, personal phones, smartphone notifications, browser notifications, it has become necessary for us to seemingly be in several different places at once. We read our emails whilst having meals, we browse social media whilst watching TV, we flick through reports whilst on the phone to colleagues. While we believe that multitasking is us being as efficient as possible, using what little time we have to get more done, could it be that multitasking is actually slowing us down? Could we get more done if we focussed on doing one thing at a time?

The answer is a resounding: YES! Yes, we could get a lot more done if we focussed on one thing at a time rather than trying to do two or more things at once. Think about the last dinner party you cooked for where you were trying to cook two or more things at once. Maybe you were searing some meat in one pan while you were making the sauce for it in another, and grilling your veggies. The whole time you're trying to wash the dishes from the starters so you don't end up with too many dishes in the sink later. Perhaps you even had a pie in the oven getting ready your dessert, so you had to keep an eye on that from time to time.

Wouldn't it have been easier, not to mention way less stressful, if you could do one thing at a time? Unfortunately the nature of catering for a dinner party means that you need to multitask and prepare a few things at once. However, for most other things in life, it does not need to be that stressful. For most things, we can take the time to do them properly by doing one thing at a time and giving each thing the attention that it deserves. This is perhaps a long way of saying that we would do much better to focus on just reading when we're reading.

So try to dismiss all your thoughts of other things when you're learning to speed read. If you are having trouble dismissing those thoughts, then reassess the environment you're using. Remember that you should find yourself somewhere quiet where you will be away from chaos, commotion and distractions. This applies for not just the initial learning process, but also later when you do have the skills to call yourself a speed reader. After all, speed reading in an appropriate environment will only make you a better speed reader. With the quiet and calm environment will come greater focus and much higher levels of concentration, so you can really zero in on what you are reading, understand it, and take in all the information that you need.

Understanding eye movement: why it is important to make fewer eye movements

Sounds crazy, right? Moving your eyes less when you're supposed to be reading. I know what you're thinking: "I'll skip this part because I'm not going to be able to do that, that is crazy!" It might sound weird, but it works, trust me. And, no, this isn't some gimmick. Actually, it relates to the point I made earlier about grouping words together to take in more information in one swoop. The average person moves their eyes from word to word, meaning that in this sentence alone you will have moved your eyes thirty-three times by the time you come to this full stop. Grouping the words together means that you might have been able to get through that sentence with only three or four eye movements, instead of thirty-three.

Have you ever thought about what happens to your eyes when they move from point to point? Each movement is known as a *saccade* and each time your optic nerve is flicked off it is known as *saccadic blindness*, or *saccadic masking*. As your eyes move the optic nerve is switched off during the process, meaning that it doesn't take in any information during that sliver of time it takes for your eyes to move to the next point. By minimizing the amount of time that your optic nerve spends in this state of saccadic masking you will be maximizing the amount of time you are looking at a piece of text, taking in the information it has to offer.

Speed Reading Techniques

Inspectional Reading

Inspectectional reading is divided into two different types of reading: skimming, and superficial. You may have heard that skim reading is not a good way to really take in information. Inspectional reading is the act of quickly evaluating whether a text is relevant to what you need from it.

Skimming means you're taking in just the title, headings, sub-headings, and key phrases just to determine whether it is what you are looking for.

Superficial reading is the act of reading through a text, but with the sole purpose of determining whether it is right for you. So, if you come across something you don't understand whilst superficially reading a text, you're not going to bother about looking it up, or reading any deeper.

Meta guiding

Remember how, as a kid, we used a finger to track the line in a book that we were reading. This helped us to stay on the right line and stopped us from getting confused. As we grew up into more confident readers we ditched this habit. Meta guiding is essentially taking up this habit again, but this time it will help us to read faster. Keep your finger moving slightly faster than you're comfortable with and this will help you to read faster.

Tracker & Pacer

Use a capped pen to underline each line that you read. This will cut down on regression, remember? Regression is where you go back and read something that you have read before. The capped pen is the tracker part of this method. The pacer is how fast you move that pen. Try to keep it to half a second per line. When you start out with this you may find that you have understood nothing of what you have just read, don't worry as this is normal. Your reflexes will get better over time. To begin with, just focus on your speed. Comprehension will come with time.

Silent reading - reducing subvocalization

Music is a great way to reduce subvocalization, if this is something that you do a lot. Listening to music while you read will help you to keep your inner voice at bay, but if it is too loud that can be a distraction. If you find music too distracting, or if it would be inappropriate, try chewing gum. Chewing chewing gum will keep you distracted, but in a way that will not impede your focus and concentration.

Expanding your focal range

I've mentioned taking in groups of words at a time, but how do you do this? Practice. You will need to train your eyes by staring at the middle of a Schultz table. Then try to work out the numbers on the left and the right of the spot that has your focus. It will take time, but you will eventually increase your focal range.

Grouping or Chunking

This is the act of reading a group of words at a time. I mentioned expanding your focal range, but you can also start by trying to take in groups of two words at a time. This is beginner level, but you only have to group, or chunk, 3-5 words to hit the medium level. Practice for 10-15 minutes daily and try not to go for difficult texts in the beginning. Initially try splitting up a sentence into parts and concentrate on reading a couple of words at a time.

What We've Learned

- We do work more efficiently when we do

one thing at a time, so don't practice speed reading whilst doing other stuff.

- Try to get away from distractions and find yourself a space where chaos doesn't reign.
- Try to minimize eye movements as minimizing saccadic masking will mean making the most of your reading time.
- There are a variety of basic techniques you can practice that will help you to read faster. Try them all out and work your way through them. Perhaps dedicate 10-15 minutes each day to one of them.

Chapter 5

VISUALIZATION TECHNIQUES

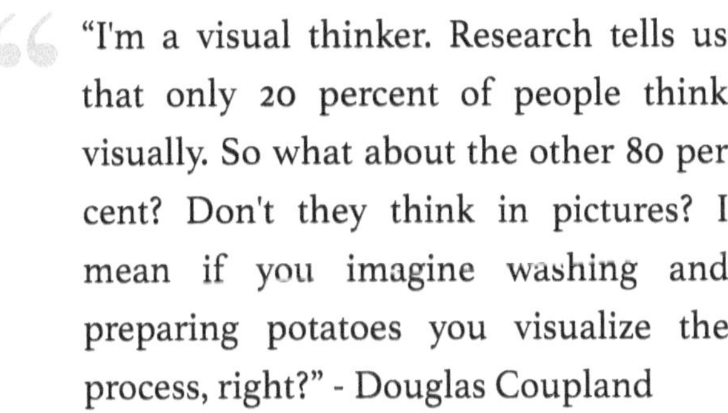

"I'm a visual thinker. Research tells us that only 20 percent of people think visually. So what about the other 80 per cent? Don't they think in pictures? I mean if you imagine washing and preparing potatoes you visualize the process, right?" - Douglas Coupland

Visualization is one of the most powerful forms of thought that we possess as humans. It gets us out of all sorts of problems and is one of our key assets when it comes to problem solving. It is one of the things that makes humans so good at problem solving and finding better ways to get things done. That is why in this chapter we are going to be looking at what makes Visualization such an important part of being human. We shall also be explaining why visualization is something that we can harness to improve our thinking processes and reading speeds.

The power of visualization

Before we start to take a good look at visualization and figure out how you can fit it into your life, we first need to understand what exactly visualization is. People go on about it, but what are they actually talking about? Well, visualization is a powerful technique that can help you to grasp and recall things that you have read, heard of felt. Ultimately you will be improving the reading speed and comprehensive ability if you learn to visualize.

Visualization is the process of creating a picture in your head of important things that you have come into contact with in medium other than seeing. Essentially, in visualizing something you are creating a mental practice run for something that you have not yet done, but will eventually do.

·   ·   ·

Normally visualization is something that we do subconsciously. However, if you can learn to do it consciously, deliberately, it is a skill that can result in you being ready to actually do the different things that you have been reading about. For example, if you can visualize building a brick wall as you are reading the steps and instructions, you will have a more solid grasp of how to actually build it. Psychologically you will have already built the wall, so when you get to actually doing you will feel like you already have the experience.

When I was preparing to take on my first clients as a personal trainer, I was surprised to find that I was not as nervous as I thought I would be. Then later, when I found out about visualization, I realized that it was because I had already been imagining what the experience would be like. Sure, I had watched others at my local gym, but I had been imagining the scenario for myself. I already had an idea of the abilities of the clients that I would be meeting and I knew what they wanted to achieve. So, I had already put together a personalized plan for each of them and I knew how I would present that plan to them. I had gone through any questions they might have, or any objections they would voice, or stumbling blocks that they would discover. So when it came to actually doing it, having conversations with them, getting them started on the gym equipment, it all went a lot smoother than I had expected. I did not know it at that time, but it was all down to the visualization process that I had unknowingly been through.

How to effectively visualize

Why is visualizing such a big deal for humans? Because we are visual creatures, we do so much through our sense of sight. Think back to the last time you were reading a novel. Did you simply read the words, or did you imagine yourself within the world created by the author's words on the page? Words and language are not natural to humans, but our sense of sight and our ability to create mental images is. Our ability to visualize is linked to our ability to create accurate mental images that reflect what we are reading. In the beginning it will feel like the activity of picturing every word you are reading is slowing you down, but with time you will get better. Remember that visualization is not just about reading more rapidly, but it is also about under-standing more.

Visualization Techniques for speed reading and comprehension

There are lots of different techniques that you can use to improve your ability to visualize while you're reading. In this section we're going to go through them so you have all the tools you need to make a success of this great skill.

Receptive Visualization

This technique is like watching a short film in your mind, and you're the director! Like many of the techniques involved in becoming a faster reader, you'll need a quiet place to concentrate, at least while you are still practicing. Start by picturing a scene vividly and add details as necessary. Add people, noises and other elements. Developing your capacity for picturing things will help you to visualize when you're reading.

Meditate

This might sound like something you don't have time for, but meditation is a powerful tool. Set aside a little time each day for meditation and you will soon be able to empty your head of thoughts and distractions, freeing your mind to imagine whatever it wants. This will help you to visualize and then you will be able to use that skill to consciously visualize while you are reading.

Visualization exercises

The above techniques are great for stimulating your ability to visualize but, if you need some additional help, here are some exercises that will make things easier for you.

Picture Exercise

This works by choosing a picture. Take a good look at it and then close your eyes and try to see it in your mind. Repeat this over and over with the same picture until you can remember most of it. This will help you to visualize.

Object Exercise

This is a great way to stimulate creativity. Yes, it may initially sound like the picture exercise, but the difference is that you will picture your chosen object in your mind and then rotate it to view it from different angles. Additionally, you can picture the surroundings. Picture the room, and details within it.

Person Exercise

Pick someone that you know really well, maybe a family member. Now try to imagine them in different places. Picture their face, their expressions, little tics, or typical actions that they do.

Place Exercise

Picture a place that you know well and place yourself in it within your mind. Bring in as many details as you can remember to make the experience as real as possible and engage all your senses. If you're at a restaurant, try to imagine people chatting around you, imagine the texture of the tablecloth, the cutlery, try to smell the aromas wafting from the kitchen.

What We've Learned

- By visualizing you will be rehearsing for something you are planning to do.

- Visualization not only helps you to read faster, but helps you to understand more.
- Effective visualization is reliant upon your capacity for imagination.
- There are different visualization techniques to suit every person.
- Different visualization exercises will help you to develop your visualization technique.

Chapter 6

HIGH-LEVEL COMPREHENSION TECHNIQUES

> "Computers allow us to squeeze the most out of everything, whether it's Google looking up things, so I guess that tends to make us a little lazy about reading books and doing things the hard way to understand how those things work." - Buzz Aldrin

I already mentioned a couple of times that being a quicker reader should not be your sole and ultimate aim. Instead, you should also be focussing on really understanding what you are reading. Sure, in the beginning you will want to concentrate on getting your reading speed up and practicing reading as quickly as possible. However, there is no point in being able to read really really fast if you are not understanding and absorbing what you are reading. As you start out with the techniques you will find that you are not retaining what you are reading because you are concentrating so much on the speed.

If you are reading this book it is because you are keen to reader faster, but don't focus on that at the expense of understanding what you are reading. Especially if you are reading because you need to learn something, as opposed to learning for pleasure. That is why this chapter is dedicated to getting you to understand what you are reading. So far we have covered the various techniques you can deploy to get yourself reading faster. Now we are going to look at the various ways you can get yourself understanding what you're reading, so you are thinking about what you are reading as you are taking it in.

These techniques are plans and steps that you can use to get the most from the text that you are reading with speed. These techniques will also help you to read faster as you will be reading with purpose when you can understand and absorb the information you are reading. By the time you have mastered these techniques you will feel empowered and in charge of your reading and learning.

Preview strategy: skim and scan your reading material

Previewing is one of the most well known ways to stimulate speed reading and most of us have done it at one point or another, usually without knowing that we were doing it. If your life sees you reading a lot of material, you have probably used the preview method to focus on sections of the text at a time. By using the previewing method you are forcing your-self to zoom in only the words and key phrases that truly matter in a piece of text. It might sound like a waste because you are only paying attention to a relatively few words, but it is an easy way to deter-mine whether the text is relevant to your needs before you invest more of your time and effort into it.

Previewing is a really good time saver but while you may have done it naturally in the past it actually takes some dedication to do it the right way. Over time you will learn how to use previewing to really zero in on the information that really matters to you in a piece of text. Take advantage of the headings and subheadings to get a gist of what each section is about and whether it will contain the information that you need. Are there any visuals that your eyes can land upon? For example, if you're reading a report there may be tables, graphs and charts that can give you the information you need. Bullet point lists and sections written in italics are also helpful and can quickly tell you whether or not a piece of text is worth spending more time on.

But how does this help you to understand more about what you are reading? Simple. By previewing you will be gaining an understanding of the text before going on to read it for real. This taste of the text will give you a greater insight setting you up for a more fulfilling read because you will already have little milestones within the text that you will be anticipating.

Improve your vocabulary

This might seem like a rudimentary suggestion, but it is still a valid one that needs to be mentioned. Obviously the better your vocabulary, the better chance you will stand of becoming an excellent speed reader. I'm not saying that you need to become Tracey Ullman's character in *Small Time Crooks* and start assiduously reading the dictionary, but there are other ways to improve your vocabulary.

There are lots of reasons why some people don't have as good a vocabulary as other people. I discussed the negative impression that some people have of reading and how that feeling might have developed from a young age. Lack of quality reading can have an impact on one's vocabulary so it might not be as rich as it could be. Take the time to read more challenging material in order to improve your vocabulary.

Actively seek out books, articles and other reading materials that will provide you a fresh reading experience and enrich your vocabulary. If you only have time to read a tabloid newspaper, try switching to a broadsheet newspaper. Yes, it may be difficult to make the adjustment, but it will be worth it when you realize that you don't need to hit the dictionary every time you come across a challenging word. Not only will you be saving time but you will also be understanding more of what you are reading.

Visualization and association strategy

Visualization and association is a technique that is usually associated with memory. Here it will help you to understand more about what you are reading, with the improved memory being an added bonus. There are three steps to using visualization and association. They are:

1. Substitute words
2. Imagination
3. Visual images

Substitute Words

This is the process by which you will create a connection between new knowledge and knowledge that you already have. This is how we learn and also how we come to understand new things. We understand what we are reading by association with things that we already know and understand. Visualization is the key skill for this.

. . .

A great example of this is by considering different countries. Most of us know where France is located, but if you had to describe its shape you might be in trouble. Describing the shape of Italy, on the other hand, is relatively easy. It looks like an over the knee boot. This is how we associate one thing with another.

You can do this with almost everything by breaking it down into a smaller, more manageable chunk and associating it with something relevant that you will understand and remember.

Imagination

Use your imagination to make unique associations. Vivid and unusual images are the best to help make associations between different things. This is a great way to remember things, and by remembering them you will stand a better chance of continuing to understand the new information long after you have read it. So, try to make your associations clear, distinct, vivid and as unique as possible. Try exaggerating, if you are struggling to find something unique. For the shape of Italy, for example, instead of just picturing a boot, make it a gigantic boot, or make it a series of boots.

Visual Images

Now is the time to make the association. Italy is famous for many things, frescoes, pasta, the Vatican, soccer. What do soccer players wear on their feet? Soccer boots. It's as simple as that.

Mind mapping

Mind mapping is another visual thinking technique that will help you to comprehend more as you get quicker at reading by creating connections between different pieces of knowledge. Mind mapping is particularly efficient when it comes to organizing factual information. It will help you to understand complex concepts by processing information quickly and accurately. Essentially mind mapping takes that information that you have been reading and turns it into instant knowledge by helping you to understand it a lot more quickly.

Take notes and summarize

This is a longer way of doing things, but it will do while you master the previous techniques. Taking notes and summarizing will reinforce what you have just read and help you to make sense of it in a way that you will find helpful.

What We've Learned

- Reading quickly is pointless if you are not understanding what you are reading.
- Having a good understanding of what you are reading will leave you feeling empowered and good about yourself.
- Previewing a text will help you to understand more by giving you a taster of what you will be reading.
- Previewing is also a good way of determining if a text will give you the information you need.
- Take steps to enrich your vocabulary. For some people the key to speed reading is a deeper vocabulary. Certainly you will understand a lot more of what you are reading.

- Visualization and association will not only help you to remember what you have learned, but it will help you to understand it better by engaging your imagination and forming connections.
- Mind mapping is a great visual tool that is becoming more relevant with the ever-growing emphasis on visual solutions.
- Taking notes as you go along might seem like something that will slow you down, but it does help you to understand more of the text that you are speed reading.

Chapter 7

REMEMBER MORE

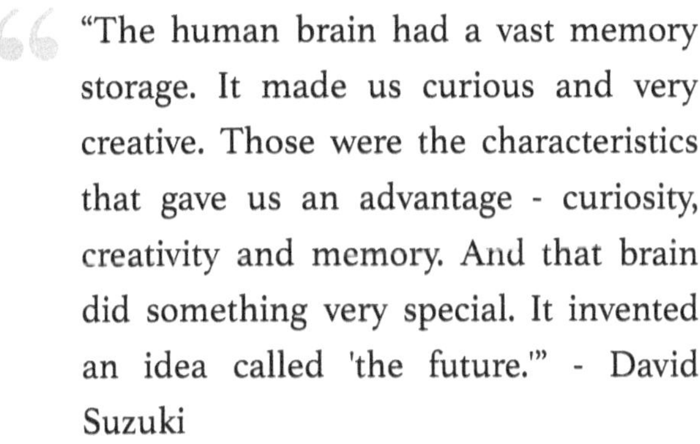

"The human brain had a vast memory storage. It made us curious and very creative. Those were the characteristics that gave us an advantage - curiosity, creativity and memory. And that brain did something very special. It invented an idea called 'the future.'" - David Suzuki

It would not be right for me to discuss speed reading without also talking about memory and what you can do to remember more of what you will be reading. After all, just as you need to understand what you are reading, you will also want to remember it. Just as there is no point in being able to read really fast if you are not going to understand what you have read, there is no point in being a speed reader if you cannot remember the information you have absorbed and the knowledge you have gained.

That is why this chapter is dedicated to giving you some top tips on good memory techniques. I know that I needed all the help that I could get when I was setting up my digital marketing business in Singapore. Not only was there a lot that I had to remember about how the still nascent digital marketing industry was working at the time, with lots of changes along the way. There was a lot to remember about how to do business in Singapore. I had to respect the customs while still being dogged about securing new business. That was one of the things that set me on the course to giving my memory skills a tune up.

Let's face it, if I could improve my memory, then I firmly believe that you can do it too. If you are going to learn to read more quickly, then a good memory is going to be crucial to your success. Not all of us were lucky enough to be born with *The X Files'* Special Agent Fox Mulder's photographic memory, the rest of us need a little help along the way and that's what I'm offering here.

How Memory Works

Perhaps the best place to start with this is in explaining how memory works. There is still a lot of research and discussion about it, but what we do know is that memory is broken down into 3 essential processes: Encoding, Storage and Recall.

Encoding

This is all of your senses working together to associate meaning with something specific. For example, you remember your fifth birthday so vividly because there was a clown making balloon animals and all your friends were there.

Storage

Your memories depend upon the strength of the connections created by the neurons, the nerve cells, within your brain. These communicate with one another and neuroscientists believe that this is what creates memories that you can access later on as either short term or long term memories.

Recall

This is where your brain attempts to bring up the information by having the relevant neurons communicate with one another. Habitually thinking of particular memories will help those connections between neurons to become stronger. Stronger connections will lead to more successful memory retrieval.

The forgetting curve

The forgetting curve is the theory behind our failure to retain information, or at least to quickly access the information we hold, about things that we don't think of very often. It is an idea that is over a hundred years old and was developed by German psychologist Hermann Ebbinghaus to determine how long it takes us to forget information.

Memory techniques for storing and recalling vast amounts of information quickly and accurately

There are so many tips and tricks for improving your memory, but most of us simply don't bother because we think it will be time consuming, or require too much effort. Here's a quick run through of some of the main ones that will improve your memory no end.

Mnemonics

Mnemonics are a really good way of remembering essential information.

Acronyms

These are an excellent way to remember fixed information. Such as Richard Of York Gave Battle In Vain, to remember the colors of the rainbow. Red, Orange, Yellow, Green, Blue, Indigo, Violet.

Musical Mnemonics

This is a powerful tool that is often used in jingles. You know the ones that you can't get out of your head after hearing it once. The most common musical mnemonic is probably the ABC song.

Rhyming Mnemonics

Rhymes create patterns that are easy to remember. One that is often used in cooking is: *looks the same, cooks the same.* That means that if you chop your veggies to the same size they should all be ready at the same time.

The Memory Palace

Perhaps the most famous proponent of the memory palace is Sherlock Holmes, the world's most famous detective. He is not wrong as the memory palace technique can be a very powerful tool. You start with the memory palace technique by choosing a place that you are very familiar with. It could be your house, or a route that you take to school, or work.

Next, place yourself in that space, in your imagination, and take a walk through the space. If it is a building, take a look into each room and walk the corridors. If it is a route to a place, take the journey and refamiliarize yourself with every aspect of it. Make a mental note of each special place of note in the building, or on your journey.

· · ·

Each special place is known as a *loci* and it is at each *loci* that you will assign a different thing that you want to remember.

Use your imagination to place an image representation of each thing you want to remember in each loci. So, for example, if you are trying to remember things that you need to take with you on your forthcoming vacation, you might try placing an image of some colorful and exotic fish in a frame on the wall above the mantelpiece in your house, to represent your snorkel. Or, you can be more outrageous and inventive. As in the last chapter, when I was discussing visualization and association, it helps to make each image as unique as possible.

Spaced Repetition

Spaced repetition is the process of introducing intervals to your studying or reading sessions. It has been proven to have positive effects on memory with individuals remembering more with intervals.

The idea is that there must be some degree of forgetting in order for us to relearn the parts that we have forgotten and thus create stronger connections between the neurons. This stronger connection creates better memories, as explained earlier in this chapter.

A study was published that determined that the optimal intervals are as follows:

1st study: 1 day

2nd study: 7 days

3rd study: 16 days

4th study: 35 days

What We've Learned

- Memory works by creating stronger connections between neurons. These connections grow stronger the more we use the particular neurons, so regularly bringing up information will help us to remember it.
- The forgetting curve outlines how quickly

we forget information once we have learned it.

- Mnemonics offer a fun way of memorizing facts and information.
- The memory palace can be a powerful and versatile memory technique, but it can take time to develop.
- Spaced repetition has been found to improve memory, but be sure to stick to your intervals.

Chapter 8

HOW TO READ A BOOK

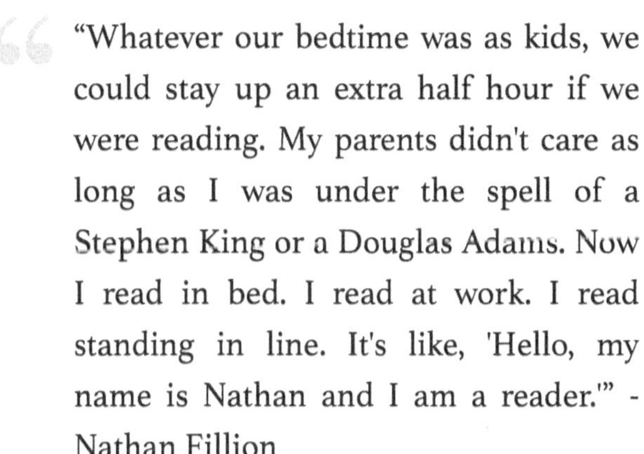

"Whatever our bedtime was as kids, we could stay up an extra half hour if we were reading. My parents didn't care as long as I was under the spell of a Stephen King or a Douglas Adams. Now I read in bed. I read at work. I read standing in line. It's like, 'Hello, my name is Nathan and I am a reader.'" - Nathan Fillion

So, we have been discussing the various techniques that you can use to become faster at reading. We have also covered the various ways you can ensure that you understand what you have been reading. Additionally we have gone over some top tips for improving your memory so you not only read information quickly, understand everything that you read to convert information into knowledge, and can remember the knowledge for later use. Now we are going to take a look at how you would use all those fascinating tips and tricks in real life to convert your speed reading journey from a dream to a reality.

It is all very well going over theories and techniques, but there is nothing like having a real life example to work from. The examples we are going to go through in this chapter will not only give you ideas about how to use the techniques we have already gone over, but they should also give you the confidence to try things out for yourself. This chapter should prove to you that these techniques and theories can work if you commit to the process and use them correctly. It won't be long until you are reading faster, understanding more and retaining your knowledge.

Reading Fiction

Many people want to read more, but they find themselves forgetting what they last read when they put down the book for a day. Part of it may be about not fully engaging with the reading process, but a big part of it will be that they simply aren't enjoying what they are reading. Maybe they find the book boring but they are persevering with it. Maybe it is the result of those negative associations they have had since childhood about not being a good reader. If this is you, you need to ignore that voice that tells you that you are not a good reader.

Also, you need to make sure that you pick something that you are going to enjoy reading. If you're not used to reading fiction, try a bunch of different genres to see what grabs you. Maybe literary fiction is more your thing.

Vocalizing

Remember that you are supposed to be minimizing the amount of effort you make so you can glide through the words more easily and smoothly. This means cutting down on reading out loud, and it also means trying not to silently say the words either.

Jumping Back

Remember that you should keep your jumping back, or regression, to a minimum. Remember that you are better than you think you are and that you don't need to read parts that you have read before. Have faith in your own abilities and know that you can keep reading without feeling that you have not understood things. Going back to re-read parts will slow you down.

Visual Thinking

As you're reading, try to process the words that you are absorbing. Use the information that the author gives you in terms of descriptions to paint the scene. This will help you to think visually and create your own version of the world that they are describing, in your mind. Remember that your brain works better with images than it does with words. Visual thinking will not only help you to read faster, but it will also help you to understand more.

Encoding, Storage, Recall

Remember the explanation about how the neurons in your brain will communicate with other, and create stronger connections? That isn't just for factual information, it works for fiction too. If you find yourself forgetting what you have read from one day to another, you need to do more to retain that information. Unlike factual information, fiction is not something that you are studying, so you are not going to re-read the information from a novel, for example. What you can do is continue to think about what you have read for some time after you have read it. Try to create a mental summary of everything you have read in the novel so far and this should create stronger memories.

Reading Non-Fiction

Preview

When you're reading non-fiction you will often be researching for something you need to learn, a report, a dissertation you need to write, or something else. Don't forget to use the preview strategy in order to quickly determine whether a text will be relevant to what you need. Seek out images that will quickly give you an idea of whether the document is right for you. Things like charts and graphs will help.

Skip Words

If you need to do more than a simple preview to discover whether an article is right for you, you could try to skip the words that are not essential to a basic understanding. This will help you to read the document quicker and allow you to determine whether it is right for you.

Spaced Repetition

It is important to not only read quickly but also to understand and retain the information that you are reading. Whether you are studying for an exam, or to retain general knowledge, spaced repetition is a powerful tool. It is not just a case of repeating the information over and over until you memorize it. Set up a schedule so you are reading or re-reading on a regular basis, but with enough of an interval so that you and your spaced repetition can fulfill its potential.

The steps on finding the main ideas from any book

Many people confuse the main ideas of a book with a summary. The two are not the same. A summary is a brief summation of what the book is about, but what we are looking at here is how to collect the ideas that inform the book.

Visual hints

Picking up on visual clues can be a great way to also pick up on what the book is ultimately about. Focus on any photographs and illustrations on the front cover of the book, or on the back cover. If the book is fiction then this might be a little trickier. But if it is a biography, for example, it should be straightforward to pick up on what the book is about from the title and the photo on the cover.

The Focus

Determine who or what is the main focus of the book. Who are the main characters? Or, what is the book about, what does it describe?

The Defining Characteristics

What are the main things of note about the main characters, or about the subject of the book? Determine what these are and you will be a step closer to identifying the main ideas.

Steps one and two

Write a brief sentence or two with your answers from the first two steps. The sentence(s) you have written will illustrate the main ideas of the book.

What We've Learned

- Don't listen to anyone, or even that little voice within you, that says that you can't read faster, or that you are a poor reader. You can be a better, faster reader.
- If you are reading fiction, pick something that you find truly interesting.
- Remember to incorporate the different techniques that we have discussed in the previous chapters.
- You don't have to use all of them at once. Figure out what works best for you and which combination gives you the best results.
- Think about what you have read for a little while after you have read it. You can think about it while you're driving, or washing the dishes. The important thing is that you

create a stronger memory by going back
over the information you have read.

- Collect together the main ideas from the
book or article that you have read as this will
help you to remember the main points more
accurately.

Chapter 9

DEVELOPING YOUR READING HABITS

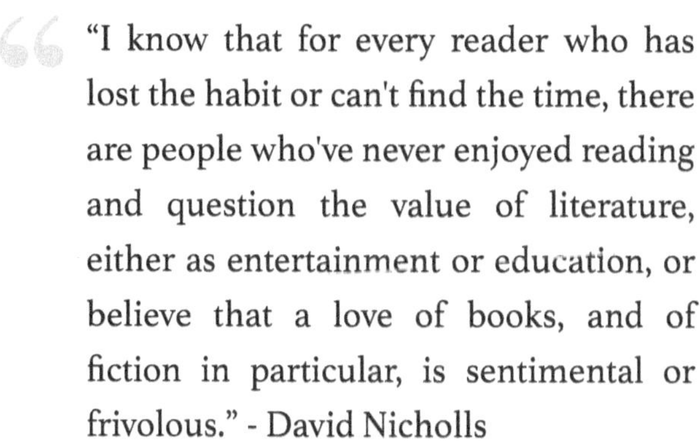

"I know that for every reader who has lost the habit or can't find the time, there are people who've never enjoyed reading and question the value of literature, either as entertainment or education, or believe that a love of books, and of fiction in particular, is sentimental or frivolous." - David Nicholls

Habits are funny things. We can try to make sense of them and change them, but it is not always guaranteed that our efforts will be rewarded. Often we will not be able to set up a strong habit, or change a bad habit because of our lack of focus, or willpower that isn't strong enough. But anything worth doing is worth doing well, and even if you do not succeed the first time in setting up a long standing habit, your perseverance will eventually be repaid. You just need to believe in yourself and ignore all the negative voices, either around you, or in your mind.

If reading, for whatever reason, has become something that you avoid, then let me tell you that you are missing out on a wonderful thing that can only enrich your life. Whether it is reading fiction, or more fact-based texts, reading has the potential to open your mind up to new experiences and broaden your horizons. All it takes is for you to take up reading as a new habit. It might initially seem like a chore, but take a few moments to shrug off that negative mindset and put yourself in a more positive frame of mind. Make the decision to make reading a part of your daily life and you will not regret it for an instant.

How to self-motivate yourself to read

Even with the best willingness in the world, you're not going to be able to establish a solid, long standing habit if you are not fully committed to the process. Making reading a habit is going to be a hard thing to do if you are already committed to doing other things in your spare time.

Of course, it is only natural that we have already well established routines for what we do in our spare time. We know what we enjoy and we make time for that. When you get back from work, you might enjoy cooking yourself a nice meal. Perhaps you enjoy watching a movie at the cinema, or your favourite show on TV. Perhaps you like to spend time chatting with your loved ones. Perhaps you like to go out to a bar and being around other people. At the weekend you might prefer to take trips, or set up family gatherings rather than read a book. What I'm trying to say is that there are lots of distractions and lots of things that many people would rather do than read, especially if they harbor negativity towards reading. What you need to do is establish your reason for wanting to read more.

Do you want to read more for yourself? Is this a decision that you made for yourself? Or are you trying to read more because someone, or something, is pressuring you? If it is because of some outside influence you will find it a lot more difficult to establish reading as a habit. What you need to do is make the decision for yourself, and why wouldn't you? There are so many good reasons to read more. If you are reading more for yourself, then you will find it so much easier to find the willpower when you are starting out.

If you have decided to make reading a habit for yourself you need to make a list of the reasons why you have chosen to do this. Do you want to find out more about a particular topic? Are you trying to learn something for work, or for school? Do you just want to read for fun? Once you have established the reasons you can focus on these and keep them in mind as you set up reading as a habit. Each time you feel your willpower fading you can think of these reasons and they will push you on to keep up your reading.

If you have a negative view of reading it might be to do with how you viewed reading from childhood. In fact so many of the ways we see things as adults are to do with our childhood encounter with them. Reading doesn't need to be a scary thing that you need to avoid. You can turn this view of it around and see reading in a more positive light. Indeed, this is something that you must do if you are going to establish reading as a habit. Shake off those old beliefs and embrace reading. It is not something that you should avoid, it is something that you should long for when you have gone too long without it.

The best way to find more time to read

Finding time to read is not always easy. Most of us who do not already have time dedicated to reading as a part of our daily lives can find it difficult to find the time. We all have so many other things going on. Some of us work some more when we get home from work. Some of us have dinner to cook for hungry families. We have laundry to do, tidying up to do, bedtime stories to read. Yes, that last one can technically count as reading, but you know what I mean.

This is where time management can be your friend. Here is a tip. Take the time to sit down with a piece of paper and map out your average week. Maybe you don't have the time to read when you get home, but you might be surprised at what other pockets of time you can find in your day. Maybe during lunch, maybe on the train journey home. If you work out, why not read whilst you're on the running machine, or exercise bike? When I was studying to become a personal trainer I would study on the way to and from my dreary office job.

I knew why I was learning and I was dedicated to it because I had become passionate about physical exercise, and desperately wanted out of my desk job. If you are dedicated you will be able to find time in your day to read. You won't necessarily have to shift things around either. It's just a case of being prepared to go the extra mile to make reading a part of your daily routine.

21 days to developing your reading habit

There is a belief out there that it takes only 21 days to form a habit. This works for some people, and not for others, but give it a go. It generally takes me longer to form a new habit, but there is no reason why you can't be better than me at it. The idea is that you stick to doing something for 21 days in a row and that by the end of that you will have fully incorporated a new habit into your daily routine.

·   ·   ·

I personally believe that it takes a little more than just that. In fact, I think you will need to avoid the other distractions that can tear you away from reading. Distractions such as TV, going out, chatting with friends. Nevertheless, this is a good suggestion that does work for some people, but put your book in a handy place and avoid giving in to distracting temptations. For example, try placing your book in the spot where you normally keep the TV remote control.

What We've Learned

- What are your reasons for wanting to read more? Establish your reasons and use these to bolster your willpower when it is flagging.
- Turn your negative attitude about reading into a positive one that will have you longing for a book when you have gone without it for too long.
- Decide to pursue reading as a habit for yourself, not because other people are trying to push you into it.
- If you find that you don't have time for reading when you get home, map out your

day into a schedule to identify any available
pockets of time.

- Try making time available for reading 21
  days in a row to form a habit, but be sure to
  remove any possible distractions and put
  your book in a convenient place.

Chapter 10

APPLYING YOUR NEW SKILLS

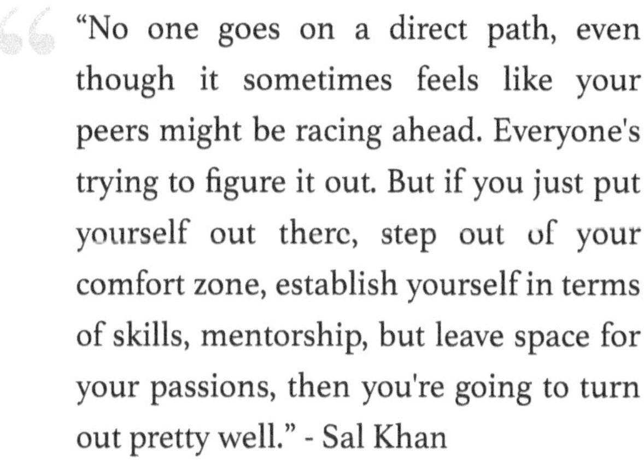

"No one goes on a direct path, even though it sometimes feels like your peers might be racing ahead. Everyone's trying to figure it out. But if you just put yourself out there, step out of your comfort zone, establish yourself in terms of skills, mentorship, but leave space for your passions, then you're going to turn out pretty well." - Sal Khan

By this point you will be keen to not only put your new skills into practice, but you will also want to measure how you are doing. Remember all those chapters ago when I suggested that you time your reading so you can know how many words you were able to read per minute? Guess what? It is now time for you to time yourself again. But this time you will be armed with a bunch of great techniques that will be speeding up not only your reading, but also your comprehension and your ability to retain the knowledge that you have gathered.

Measuring how quickly you are reading now may seem like a scary prospect, but this is the only way to know how much progress you have made. If you have become a lot quicker, then that is absolutely brilliant! But don't worry if it seems like you have not made much progress and are not reading much quicker than you were at the beginning of reading this book. The techniques will take a while to embed themselves and it will take a while for you to become better at incorporating them as part of your regular reading habits. So, there is no need to fear the results of measuring yourself. On the contrary, whatever the results, you will have a new goal to aim for because you should always be aiming to become faster and faster. If you have not guessed already, this chapter is all about tracking your progress and setting new goals.

How to track your progress

Of course, the easiest way to determine how much progress you believe you have made is to use a stopwatch to discover how long it has taken you to read, say, a hundred words. Alternatively, again using your stopwatch, you could count how many words you can read in a minute. This would give you an accurate idea of your words per minute. Remember that you are supposed to be doing this with a text that you have not read before, so no cheating with something you have read dozens of times before. If you do that you'll only be cheating yourself.

Some people time themselves daily. This is a great way to keep yourself motivated and push yourself to read faster each time. Although, you should remember that speed reading is a long term endeavour. It is unlikely that you will make significant gains from one day to the next. If you can withstand the suspense you could try measuring your progress with longer intervals. This is what I did when I was learning to speed read and maybe it is the geek in me, but I have to say that I found it exciting to measure how quickly I was reading a week or two weeks after the last time I checked. Not only was it something to look forward to, but it was something that pushed me to practice more during the intervals.

I mentioned before that you will have to adjust the way you speed read to incorporate different techniques until you find something that works for you. Measuring your progress is a way of determining which techniques are working best for you. Remember that it is not just one technique that will get you reading faster. You will have to use them in combination so you are not just reading faster, but understanding more to turn information you are reading into knowledge, and then retaining that knowledge.

As I said, it is important that you not only read faster, but comprehend and remember more, so something else that you can do to measure your progress with speed reading is to set yourself a little test. Give yourself a passage to read in a minute. Make a note of where you reach at the minute mark and then put the passage away. Half an hour later get yourself a pen and a sheet of paper and then try to write down as much as you can remember. Try to explain any complex theories, or arguments within your writing.

Next, go back to the passage and count the number of words you read up to the end of the minute. This will not only give you your words per minute score, but it will also give you a better idea of how much you are understanding and able to remember to write down half an hour later. I will bet that you will do much better than you think you will.

Setting goals

No matter what you are doing, whether it is taking up exercise or dieting, it is always tempting to set yourself a high target from the outset. The reasons are twofold. You want to do well. Also, you want to be naturally good at it so it doesn't feel like a chore. The truth is that anything worth doing will take time to accomplish. So set yourself reasonable goals. Start off with the goal of improving your words per minute by ten words the next time you measure yourself. Then try increasing that goal by twenty words. After that you should have a good enough idea of the progress you are making to adjust your goals accordingly.

Applying your skills in daily life

You will find that there is almost no end to the areas in your everyday life where you can use your new speed reading skills. Use them at school to write reports, use them at work to understand new directives, use them in the kitchen to read ingredients, understand the processes and remember the steps as you cook for a dinner party. How about that home improvement project you have always wanted to do? Read up on how to build that brick barbecue and then get out there and do it!

What We've Learned

- Don't be afraid to measure your progress as knowing how you are doing is the only way to adjust your approach.
- Whether you are reading a lot faster or have made a small improvement, you will be able to alter your goal for speed reading and aim for a faster time.
- It will take time to incorporate the different techniques, so don't become disheartened if you think you have not made much progress.

- Find out your words per minute by using a stopwatch to see how many words you can read in a minute, but be sure not to use a text that you have read before.
- Don't forget to track your understanding and how much you remember as well.
- Be sensible about setting goals and start off with a modest goal before adjusting it accordingly.
- Your skills can be used in a whole range of different ways, not just for writing essays. Don't be shy about using them in all different parts of your life.

Chapter 11

BONUS CHAPTER: READING TIPS & TOOLS

Remember that speed reading is a skill that will develop with time. None of us have a magic wand that will get us reading faster overnight, so don't become despondent if you don't immediately see positive results. I understand that the process can be frustrating for you, just as it was for me when I first embarked upon my speed reading journey. That is why I have put together something that I didn't have when I was learning to speed read: a wealth of extra tips and tools that will help you along the way.

Studying for exams

My best tip on studying for exams is to adopt the SQ3R, or SWRRR, method. It stands for:

- Survey
- Question
- Read
- Recite
- Review

This is particularly helpful if you need to read and understand entire chapters and works like this.

Survey

Before reading the chapter, take a few moments to fully take in the title, subtitle, headings, subheadings, captions under pictures and images, Take a quick read through any introductory and concluding passages, as well as any supporting notes and guides.

Question

Whilst performing the first step, surveying, begin turning everything you are reading into questions. Ask yourself questions about the headings and subheadings. Ask yourself what they could mean. Begin asking yourself what you already know about this chapter, ask yourself what your teacher or lecturer has already told you about this.

Read

As you read, answer the questions that you asked yourself. Make note of every italicized word, bolded phrase. Take a good look at any images included within the chapter. Everything in your book is there to help you so try to take it all in.

Recite

Try to create an oral summary of everything that you have just read without looking through the chapter again. Then go through the text again and make notes about it, but be sure to put the information in your own words rather than just copying it from the book. Remember to speak out loud as using your senses helps you to learn.

Review

This is an ongoing exercise that you need to do regularly to keep the knowledge fresh in your mind. Read through the chapter again covering parts of it to test yourself. Create flashcards using your own words.

Recite out loud what you know from the chapter. Alternative all these different methods of revision every so many days to keep things fresh.

Active Reading

Being an active reader means thinking about what you are reading, not just mindlessly getting through the words. It also means being ready to take action. Here are some tips and questions that will help you succeed in active reading:

1. Why are you reading what you are reading? Will there be a test soon? An exam? Do you need to write a report of some sort? Is it to qualify for a promotion at work?
2. Always create some questions that you will answer by reading through the text. This gives you extra motivation for reading, the process of finding something out.
3. Always read with a pen in your hand, ready for taking notes, for underlining words and key phrases that you either don't know, or know will be important to remember.
4. Teach someone else what you have learned. It could be that you tell your partner about

it, or your friends, but actively thinking the information through and the process of explaining it to someone else will help you to understand it better and also to remember it.

Reading a book a week

If you are trying to rise to the challenge of reading a book in a week, and eventually 52 books in a year, this is my list of tips for getting you through the challenge.

1. Always read as soon as you wake up in the morning. Set your alarm an extra half hour early so you can stay in bed reading.
2. Try to always have your book with you so you can take advantage of any extra time that comes your way. These days it is so easy to have a digital copy of a book on your phone, or tablet, while you are commuting, waiting for someone, in line at the supermarket.
3. If it's a novel that you are reading, make sure that you actually like it. Don't just read it because it's on a list of "books you need to

read before you die", or something. If you find the book boring, don't be afraid to ditch it. Time wasted on a book you dislike is time stolen from a book you will love.

4. If you don't have time to read on one day, make up for it by reading more the next day.

5. Remember that it is important to try to use all your senses when speed reading, and an audiobook can be a great way to use your sense of hearing. You can even use this for studying since it would be another way to preview the text.

6. Joining a book group is a great way of motivating each other to read more and read enough to talk about the book at the following meeting.

Other tips

- Reduce eye strain by taking a break every thirty to sixty minutes.
- Use earplugs to cut down on noise distraction while you're practicing speed reading, and always practice in a quiet and well-lit space.
- Always make sure that you are

understanding what you are reading, rather than solely concentrating on reading at speed.

- If you wear glasses make sure that the lenses are clean and free of scratches.
- If you need to read something that is complex, try to read it when you are most alert, such as in the morning.

Popular Speed Reading Apps and Tools

There exist a range of apps that can help you to read faster. These vary in their levels of helpfulness, and it depends upon each individual whether the app works for them or not. Here's a few of them.

1. Spreeder CX: This can be used either on iOS or via your browser, offers different reading modes to choose from, as well as training that helps to cut down on regression and other bad habits.
2. The 7-Speed Reading App: This app is available to use through your browser and includes a wide and comprehensive range video tutorials to offer you a visual guide to all the different techniques.

3. ReadMe! App: This app helps you to read faster by highlighting in red a group of words. This helps by encouraging you to focus on the group of words and not regress, or become distracted. It's available on Android and iOS.

AFTERWORD

Thank you for taking the time to read my book, and I genuinely wish you all the luck in the world on your speed reading adventure. As I have said several times in this book, speed reading is not something that happens overnight, or even over a month. It is a continual process because you can always get faster at reading. Even when you are reading twice as fast as you did before getting serious with the techniques included in this book, you should still be eager to improve and become faster. Why? Because that is human nature. We should not be content to sit back and rest on our laurels. We should always be eager to push the envelope and get better at doing things.

However, as I have said before, remember that becoming a faster reader is not the only important factor here. Yes, it may have been the reason why you came across this book, but my aim has not solely been to get you to read faster. I have also given you some choice tools for understanding more about what you are reading. You should also benefit from the memory techniques that we have discussed in order to retain more of the knowledge.

Remember that the words on the page are meaningless without analysis and understanding. It is your analysis and understanding that will convert those words into information and knowledge. Of course, there is no point doing any of this if you are not going to remember it, right? That's why it was so important to include memory improvement techniques within this book as well.

Regression is something that many people do. Often they believe that they have not understood something clearly, or have skipped a section, so they go back and read something that they have already read. This slows down our reading speed and actually impairs our ability to understand, leading us to regress, a cycle of inefficiency. Remember that when you vocalize you are diverting resources from actually reading to moving your lips and your tongue. Even if you are sub-vocalizing you are still distracting yourself by doing something that is not necessary, dramatically slowing down your reading speed.

If you have never had much confidence and always considered yourself a poor reader, you should keep in mind that reading is something that is not natural to humans. We are beings that find it easier to process visuals and images. That is why visualization can be such a powerful tool. Learn to use it correctly and it will be a magnificent method to have you tearing through text in record time. Becoming a visual thinker involves a learning process that will eventually allow you to add the visual element to your reading, not only speeding up your reading, but also your comprehension of what you are reading.

Remember to put into practice the memory improvement techniques that we discussed. If you can make the memory palace method work for you I will be really impressed. It took me a long while to get it to work for me, but it is worth the amount of time and effort. It can have such a hugely positive effect on your life and it really is a skill that can touch every corner of your life, just like many of the techniques and methods mentioned in this book. Everything mentioned here is something that can support you in areas other than those you wanted to improve.

No matter what we do in life there are always those who will try to bring us down and tell us that we are not good enough, or are wasting our time doing the wrong thing. Do not listen to those people. Many of them will simply be jealous that you are trying to better yourself. Some of them will be upset that you are improving your life while they do not have the motivation to do the same for themselves. Sometimes that voice telling us that we are no good and that we should quit is that little nagging, negative voice in our mind that is always there to kick us when we are down. We all have one, so do not be shy about admitting it, but do not be afraid to ignore it either.

Yes, the road to becoming a faster reader will be a long one that may be tough going in the beginning, but I believe in you and I know that you will eventually find the process very rewarding and fulfilling. Remember all those chapters ago when I asked you to be honest about your reasons for wanting to become a faster reader? Well, improving yourself and bettering your life is only one of the reasons why you should be doing this. Another reason is that you should be excited to discover what you can do, and then find ways to surpass it.

As humans we are constantly surprising, and as individuals we have the ability to surprise not only each other but ourselves. Remember that you do not know what you are truly capable of until you try. So try, that is all I ask of you. Try to stick to the techniques explained in this book and work with them all until you find your optimal combination of methods that yield results for you. Once you have found something that works for you, by all means work your chosen methods, but do not be afraid to experiment. Above all, remember that reading is not a chore, it is one of the most wonderful ways of communicating that humans have. There is a whole world of beauty and culture and knowledge. It is all out there waiting for you, so don't let anything or anyone hold you back. Be the best that you can be and never stop trying to improve yourself. Be determined and show us all what you can do. I am always excited to see what others will do with the benefit of my knowledge that I have accrued throughout my life and career. So go ahead and surprise me!

AUTHOR'S NOTE

Thank you so much for taking the time to read my book. I hope you have enjoyed reading this book as much as I've enjoyed writing it. If you enjoyed this book, please consider leaving a review on Amazon. Your support really means a lot and keeps me going.

If you want more resources like this, follow me on my author profile on Amazon. You will find useful free tools for self development and success that will help you 10X your results.

ABOUT THE AUTHOR

Steven Hopkins is a personal trainer, entrepreneur, life coach, and author on a mission to awaken people to their innate talents and purpose so they can leave their mark in the world.

Steven holds a Master's degree in Behavioral Science and specializes in the areas of success, motivation, self-discipline, communication, NLP techniques, psychology, and human behavior.

When he isn't helping his clients attain their maximum potential, Steven Hopkins enjoys meditating, playing extreme sports, and traveling across the globe. He also loves spending quality time with his lovely wife and his two beautiful children.